THE GHOSTLY TALES OF

SNOHOMISH

Published by Arcadia Children's Books
A Division of Arcadia Publishing
Charleston, SC
www.arcadiapublishing.com

Spooky America is a trademark of Arcadia Publishing, Inc.

First published 2021

ISBN 978-1-5402-4940-1

Library of Congress Control Number: 2021938356

Notice: The information in this book is true and complete to the best of our knowledge. It is offered without guarantee on the part of the author or Arcadia Publishing. The author and Arcadia Publishing disclaim all liability in connection with the use of this book.

All images courtesy of Shutterstock.com.

Spooky America

THE
GHOSTLY TALES
OF
SNOHOMISH

SALOON

DEBORAH CUYLE

Adapted from *Haunted Snohomish* by Deborah Cuyle

arcadia
CHILDREN'S BOOKS

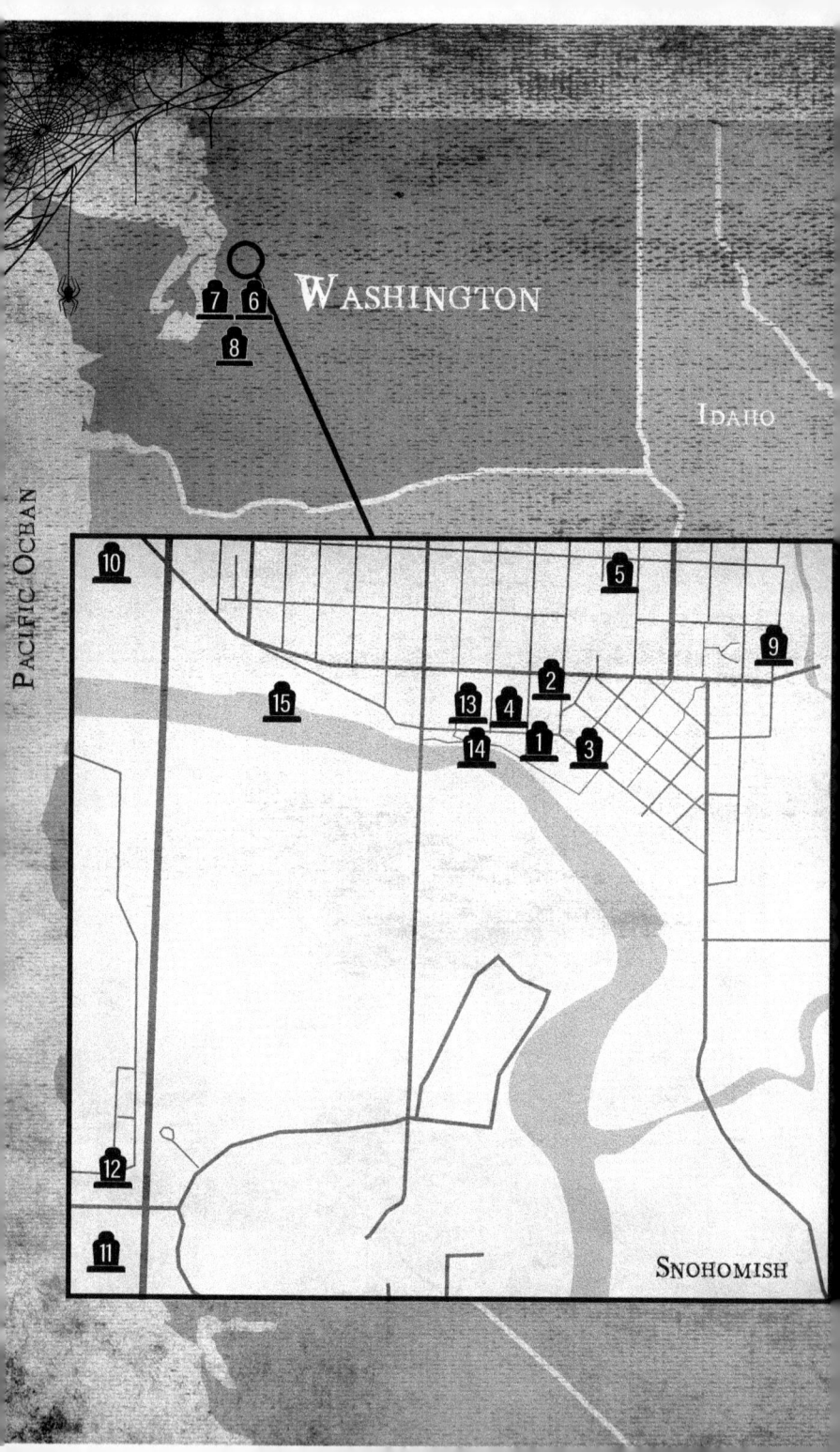

WASHINGTON

IDAHO

PACIFIC OCEAN

SNOHOMISH

TABLE OF CONTENTS & MAP KEY

Introduction 3

1. Chapter 1. The Ghosts of the Oxford Saloon 7

Chapter 2. Downtown Snohomish Ghosts 19
    2. The Cabbage Patch

Chapter 3. Catherine and Her Haunted Library 31
    3. Carnegie Library

Chapter 4. Snohomish's Haunted Old Jail 39
    4. The Marks Building

5. Chapter 5. The 1886 Haunted Maughlin Mansion 49

Chapter 6. The Miserable Man and His Fiddle 59
    6. Fiddler's Bluff
    7. Kenwanda Golf Course

Chapter 7. Haunted Cemeteries of Snohomish 67
    8. Maltby Cemetery
    9. Pioneer Cemetery
    10. GAR Cemetery

Chapter 8. The Haunted Corn Mazes and Farms 81
    11. Thomas Family Farm
    12. Stalker Farms

Chapter 9. Railroad Ghosts 89

Chapter 10. Other Snohomish Haunts 95
    13. Fred's Rivertown Alehouse
    14. 1107 First Street
    15. Snohomish River

Introduction

If you want to see or hear a real "live" ghost, look no further than the small town of Snohomish. Why? Because it truly would be a miracle if you *didn't* see a ghost ... almost every building along First Street in Snohomish has a story or legend that will give you the chills—either while reading about them or (if you are brave enough) when you encounter them.

You might meet the ghost of the policeman Henry who was killed at the Oxford Saloon. Maybe you will feel the light touch of an invisible child's hand as you enjoy a slice of pie at the Cabbage Patch. And if you are feeling really brave, the spirits who roam the cemeteries in town might just appear before your eyes as you walk among the tombstones!

You might hear the phantom clippity-clop of horses' hooves on the streets late at night when there are no horses around. Is this sound the ghostly echo of one of the horse-drawn carriages that filled the streets in the 1900s? You might see the red-haired Irish ghost that pops in and out of stores downtown. What does he want? No one really knows.

If you visit Snohomish close to Halloween, you might get a fright when you visit haunted corn mazes. You may encounter the ghost of a farmer killed nearby long ago. His spirit still wanders in the fields late at night, begging for someone to help him.

Keep your eyes and ears open in every building or landmark you visit. Be prepared to be spooked at least once—or hopefully twice! If you can't visit Snohomish in person, then snuggle up beside a warm fire with your best friend or a family member and read all about the dead people who refuse to leave the spooky little town.

But beware ... some people say that if the ghostly spirits like you they might try to follow you home!

The Ghosts of the Oxford Saloon

The Oxford Saloon building was built between 1889 and 1890. The ghosts moved in soon after. Walk down the rickety wooden stairs that lead to the basement, and you will most likely feel an invisible hand touch the side of your face. Next, the hairs on the back of your neck will rise up, alerting you that a ghost is nearby.

Who is this mysterious ghost? A friendly cop named Henry from the late 1890s died on this staircase. The legend goes that he haunts the Oxford because he is angry his killer was never captured. Henry still roams the basement, determined to someday catch his murderer and bring him to justice.

Back in the old days, police did not have fingerprint databases or DNA testing like they do now. They had to work very hard to crack a case or solve a murder. Sometimes a simple clue would lead to a killer. A strange and unique button might be found under a chair at the crime scene—the very same kind of button that was also missing from a suspect's shirt. There might be a mark in the dirt from a boot or shoe where a murder took place. The pattern of the sole would have to match a suspect's boots in order to solve the crime.

What questions would a policeman from the 1900s ask himself? He might wonder if the boot print belonged to a man or a woman. He would judge the size of the feet. Was it a working person's boot or an expensive one that only the rich could afford? All of these small pieces of evidence had to be collected to solve the crime. If the policeman didn't have a watchful eye, he might miss an important piece of the puzzle. If that happened, the crime might not be solved. The killer might never be found. What kinds of clues would you search for if you were a policeman back then?

Now, back to our story about the ghost of Henry, the Snohomish policeman. In the 1900s, the Oxford Saloon looked much like it does today—pretty, stained-glass windows, heavy doors, and a tall wooden front—a perfectly inviting atmosphere for an old ghost to feel right at home!

One murky and foggy night as officer Henry was working security, a fight broke out between two men. As they struggled and hit each other, Henry tried to break up the dispute. One man had a knife and accidentally stabbed Henry instead of his opponent. When he realized what he had done, the man ran away as fast as he could into the dark night air.

Shocked and frightened, Henry held his stomach as blood oozed from the wound. The red liquid dripped down the stairs one step at a time until it pooled onto the basement floor. Henry staggered and sat down on one of the steps, calling for help, knowing it was probably too late. Geesh, he was only trying to do his job!

People in the tavern ran out into the street and called for a doctor, hoping poor Henry could be saved. Help finally came, but it was too late. Henry bled to death on the stairs.

Today, the ghost of Henry still roams the

stairs. Visitors to the tavern hear creaks on the wooden steps as he walks up and down, still searching for justice over 100 years later. Is he angry that his murderer was never sent to the gallows? Is he protecting the patrons, just as he did when he was alive? Or is Henry simply just wandering the building because it is his favorite place to be in Snohomish? Most believe that Henry is still trying to apprehend his mysterious assailant. His murderer was never found.

It seems a policeman's work never ends! *Even in death.*

Henry is not the only ghost at the Oxford Saloon. There is a mysterious gentleman who wears a dark suit and a bowler hat (a hard felt hat with a distinctive round rim that was popular in the old days). Who could this ghost be? It might be the original owner of the building, Arthur Blackman. Along with his brother, he started a lumber mill in town in 1883. Later, he ran a dry goods store out of the building.

Others feel this well-dressed spirit might be the distinguished Snohomish architect from that era, J.S. White, who designed the Oxford building. White was a very busy and successful man in Snohomish. He designed many homes and buildings in town, and today, tours are given to show off his incredible work. There is a good chance White's ghost *is* haunting Snohomish—he is probably still admiring his craftsmanship!

There are two more ghosts wandering around the Oxford. The upstairs section still has a private door that leads to a room where a young woman was killed. Her tragic spirit still haunts the place.

The ghost was named Amelia. Her story has many different versions. Most people believe she was murdered inside the closet in Room Six. At least that's where they found her cold body one morning. People who visit the building can smell her lavender perfume in the hallway.

Sometimes a chair will move by itself or a small object will be thrown off a desk by an unseen hand. Is Amelia trying to get somebody's attention? Many people have seen her shadowy figure lurking in the closet

where her body was discovered. Some ghost hunters have even captured her eerie spirit in photographs! No one knows exactly how Amelia died. They do not know if she was murdered, committed suicide, or died from natural causes. Her death remains a mystery even today. One thing is for sure though: she does not want to be forgotten and makes sure everyone knows that she is still there.

The spirit of a woman named Katherine also haunts the Oxford. Tenants have reported that lights constantly flicker on and off.

Old-time music plays faintly from out of nowhere. The smells of tobacco and perfume come and go. Not much is known about Katherine, except that her apparition is frequently seen. She is dark-haired, thin, and very beautiful. She is seen wearing elaborate dresses with long, flowing skirts and fancy hats. Unusual cold spots can be felt on the main floor and then just as quickly disappear. Are these the signal or proof of her ghostly presence?

There was once an old doll on the top of the bar at the saloon. Its creepy eyes would open and close by themselves. Some people claim to have even seen the doll's head mysteriously move and wink one glass

eyeball. So many people were frightened by the scary doll that it is now kept hidden. Nothing is creepier than a doll that somehow moves all by itself!

The Oxford is considered one of the most haunted places in the state of Washington, and people come from all over the United States to visit it. In 2015, the Oxford even caught the attention of the famous show *Ghost Adventures*, with Zak Bagans and his crew!

Historical District of Snohomish

Downtown
Snohomish Ghosts

The building known as the Cabbage Patch Restaurant on Avenue A was erected in 1905. The structure had previously been a boardinghouse and an antique store.

The Cabbage Patch is adorned with elegant wrought iron fencing on its balconies and a front yard full of flowers, but its past reflects a different atmosphere. The beautiful, two-story

Victorian house has seen its fair share of tragedies through the years.

There have been so many fires in town that over the years some people actually believe a nasty spirit has to be involved, acting as a phantom arsonist. There were two massive fires in 1893, destroying several stores on the street. During a horrible fire in 1911, thirty-five buildings burned to the ground! Several people died during these fires, and it is believed that their agitated spirits still roam the streets of Snohomish. Luckily, during this fire, the Cabbage Patch only suffered minimal damage.

But in 2004, the Cabbage Patch wasn't so lucky. It caught fire, and the flames also threatening nearby homes and businesses. The building was destroyed and had to be completely rebuilt. The owner tried to recreate the old building's facade as much as possible to retain its original character. Even though the old Cabbage Patch is gone, the ghosts remain.

The most famous downtown ghost is a young girl named Sybil Sydney, who died in 1930 and haunts the Cabbage Patch building. Almost everyone has seen the restless spirit of Sybil, a dark-haired 11-year-old girl who is said to have tragically plunged to her death on the steps leading down to the dining room.

Sybil wanders on both floors of the building but likes to hang out on the stairs where she died.

How did she die? One local legend states that Sybil was walking down the stairs one night when she accidentally tripped, her small body cascading down to the bottom of the landing where she lay motionless. She had broken her neck, and the accident killed her instantly.

But there are several different, more-sinister versions of the legend of Sybil.

Another story says that a young girl named Sybil lived in the building with her family during the mid-1900s. Her uncle also lived with them, but he mostly stayed upstairs. People in town did not like her uncle much. He was a bit of a bully and often mean to people. Sybil and her uncle are said to have gotten into a fight, and he angrily shoved Sybil down the stairs, where she broke her neck and died. Her spirit is said to roam the building, seeking revenge on her uncle for killing her. Some say Sybil's uncle also haunts the space. His sandy-haired ghost has been seen wearing a dark jacket and roaming the rooms. Why does *he* haunt the Cabbage Patch? Does he feel sorry for what he did and now wants Sybil to forgive him? Not much is known about her uncle or why he may have killed his niece.

Another part of Sybil's story includes a young boy who lived next door to the Cabbage Patch. He was often found talking and playing with an invisible person in his backyard. His concerned mother asked the boy who he was talking to, as she saw no one there.

"I am playing with Sybil," he said simply. "She hurt her neck when she fell down the stairs." His alarmed mother was shocked

and did not know what to say. There was no way this boy could have known the story of Sybil and her death.

Some see Sybil's apparition walking up and down the stairs where she died, wearing a long white dress. She seems to be searching for someone or something. Others see the lace curtains moving when the windows are closed tight. Employees see glasses and plates move and crash to the ground.

Sybil's ghost has also been seen near the pie case; her spirit accompanied by the sound of her laughter. Sometimes the girl is also seen with the ghost of a friendly collie dog. If you are in the dining room, you might see her out of the corner of your eye, the dark-colored pooch at her heels. Many say they feel the furry warmth of a dog rubbing against their legs as they eat dinner. Is the ghost dog begging for a treat? A second dog also haunts the Cabbage Patch. This dog is a small terrier type. The faint sounds of his barking and clawing can be heard near the kitchen or back room. He is sometimes seen with the ghost of an older woman.

Upstairs, the restaurant gets even creepier. A jukebox that does not work (and isn't even plugged in to an outlet) starts playing mysterious music. Is it the ghost of Sybil playing her favorite tunes?

The ghost of a young, beautiful girl named Clara Blanche Gillespie haunts downtown Snohomish. Her family moved to Snohomish County from Michigan. One day in 1897, she came to town in a horse-drawn carriage in

search of the perfect wedding dress for her marriage to a Mr. Braaten, whose first name has been lost in the passing of time. The happy couple looked forward to starting their life together. But the wedding and the perfect life would not happen.

The couple's carriage stopped on First Street so their horse could get fresh water, but there was a problem with the horse's bridle. Mr. Braaten decided to remove the headstall and adjust the bit. The mare became frightened and started to run away. The horse was spooked. It was impossible to control her. Mr. Braaten was dragged for several yards behind the carriage as he tried to rein her in. Inside the carriage, Clara was jostled and thrown from the rig. She landed hard on the rocky street.

Her fiancée ran to her side to help, but when he approached, he saw that Clara was unconscious. There was a small pool of blood behind her head where it had struck the hard surface. He took her to a nearby house to rest until a doctor could attend to her. The doctor arrived too late. Clara never regained consciousness and died with Mr. Braaten at her side.

The heartbroken Mr. Braaten never forgave himself for the loss of his bride. Now the ghostly couple can sometimes be seen together late at night, peacefully walking the streets, holding hands. Their spirits stop now and then to peer in a storefront window as if still shopping for the perfect wedding dress.

Clara's tombstone can be found in the Pioneer Cemetery next to Collector's Choice Restaurant. Some who have taken photographs of Clara's tombstone report a shiny, glowing light that radiates from the monument. Is the glow symbolic of her angelic, innocent nature and untimely death or simply a trick of the light?

The ghost of a red-haired man with a thick moustache also explores downtown Snohomish. This spirit is known as Chester Billington. He is rumored to have been killed in the area by a fatal blow or gunshot wound to his head. Although no one knows exactly why Chester's ghost roams the streets and buildings of Snohomish, one thing is certain— he does not plan on leaving anytime soon! His ghost pops in and out of the buildings in town. Ghost hunters revealed that Chester had been stationed on one of the islands in the Pacific held by the Japanese during World War II. They believe he came back to Snohomish to be close to his family and friends. He frequently moves from building to building along Avenue A, searching for them. Quick flickers of Billington's ghostly apparition happen all over town in Snohomish.

Catherine and Her Haunted Library

Nestled in a grove of trees on the east side of town, there is an abandoned library that's home to a very active ghost named Catherine McMurchy.

The Carnegie Library, at 105 Cedar Avenue in Snohomish, was commissioned and built between 1909 and 1910. It was one of thousands of libraries built across the country with money donated by industrialist Andrew Carnegie.

Carnegie was an immigrant from Scotland who grew up poor but became the world's richest man. Because education was important to him, he committed much of his fortune to building libraries.

In Snohomish, a group of ambitious women dedicated to children's literature teamed up with another local club to bring a Carnegie Library to town. The library became an important part of Snohomish life.

Catherine was a local grade-school teacher before she became the town's librarian. She was a librarian from 1923 to 1939 and everyone in town loved and respected her. She lived at 429 Cedar, not far from the library. She worked tirelessly to keep the library in tip-top shape. Privately, during her life, Catherine suffered great losses. One after the other her parents and all three of her siblings died in Snohomish, leaving her alone. One by one, their bodies were taken back to North Dakota to be buried in the family plots. Alone, Catherine immersed herself in her work at the library.

She eventually retired from her beloved position at the Carnegie library. She died in

1956 at age 85, but her spirit continues to work in the library, refusing to leave it.

After her death, the library continued to operate without her, but her absence was felt by everyone. Later, the old card catalogue system was replaced with computers and the internet, something Catherine would not live to experience.

During the late 1990s, it was obvious that Snohomish had outgrown the Carnegie library. A larger modern library would be built in town, leaving the old one vacant.

But even before the library closed in 2003, many patrons experienced seeing the shadowy figure of an older lady roaming the halls, reshelving books, and looking out the windows. She often is seen wearing a large hat and a blue dress—an outfit Catherine was known to wear when she was alive. The old library was used occasionally for local events until 2017, when it was deemed dangerous and was closed for good.

Now Catherine would be all alone in the building. This is when passersby began to notice her sweet face staring out the windows from above. Did she yearn for the sounds of children's laughter to fill the library again? The dead silence was probably enough to even drive a ghost crazy!

The building is so haunted that local newspaper and library patrons bought a webcam hoping to capture Catherine's silhouette in photographs. Some wispy images were captured on film. Could the smoky-looking outline be the ghost of Catherine?

Most of the paranormal activity in the library happens upstairs. Everyone agrees that Catherine's spirit is a friendly ghost, not a scary one. Working at the library was her passion, and obviously she enjoyed it so much that she continues to work there even after her death!

Not all ghosts have to be frightening. Today, Catherine would be very happy and proud, as the Carnegie building is being restored after decades of planning. She would certainly love the sparkly and incredible seven-foot-tall crystal chandelier from 1915 that hangs inside.

A second building housing an art gallery was attached to the library. Countless artists and customers heard the voice of a woman when no one was there. They saw objects move on their own and heard footsteps clomping up and down the stairs when no one else was in the room. People working in the building felt unexplained chills.

Former Snohomish librarian Mike Malone believes Catherine's presence may be felt because she is sad. He discovered that she had been buried with no grave marker. In 2002, he funded a tombstone for Catherine that had inscribed on it, "Cherished Snohomish Librarian." She is buried at Seattle's Evergreen-Washelli Cemetery, finally getting the recognition she deserves!

CHAPTER 4

Snohomish's Haunted Old Jail

The Marks Building at 1024 First Street is perhaps the second most haunted place in Snohomish. The property had a special claim to fame: Snohomish's first flushing toilet was located here!

Built in 1888, the massive brick and stone building that sits on the corner of First and Avenue B was almost immune to destruction by fire. In 1911, a horrible fire destroyed most of the town. Luckily, most of the Marks Building was saved.

Early on, a man named John Otten ran a dry goods store there. In his store, he sold such items as fabric and clothing, tools, flour, tobacco, and sugar. Each day, he lined the shelves with products he felt the townspeople would need and enjoy. But Otten could not keep up on his lease payments, and his store eventually closed. Tom Marks soon took over the building. He wanted everyone to know he was the owner, so he had a mason carve his

name over the stone entryway. The carving is still there today.

During the 1890s, the Marks Building became the county jail. It would be home to many prisoners over the years. Snohomish was a very rough-and-tumble town in its early years. Gun slinging and bar-room brawls would occur nightly, keeping the police busy and the citizens frightened. Many Snohomish men found their way inside the jail in town where they awaited their trials. Some men had to fear execution due to their crimes. The building would remain the county jail until the late 1890s.

The basement of the building still has the original stone-arched jail cells. The only light that reached the prisoners here was through the purple glass squares set in the sidewalk above (you can still see them today). Conditions for the prisoners were terrible. It is rumored that there was not enough money to provide food for the inmates. Could this be one of the reasons many believe there are phantom prisoners here now and why they are so angry?

Years after the jail closed, Raymond Harmon took over the building and created a department store that sold clothing for both men and women. For many years, the Harmon family ran a successful store simply called Harmon's Department Store. The Harmons moved their store to another location in 1964. Did they move their store because of ghosts, or did they just want a smaller space? It is a mystery.

To this day, there is so much ghostly activity in this building, it's unbelievable. Everyone who rents a space or works there has had a ghostly experience.

People who find their way to the basement of the Marks Building hear the sound of jangling keys. Perhaps it's the ghosts of former prison guards? They hear moans and screams coming from nowhere. The sound of metal cups being run along the metal bars of a cell grates through the basement. The elevator in the building moves from floor to floor with no

one is in it, sometimes when it is locked! No one knows the identity of spirits who haunt the jail.

Could one spirit be a man murdered on the night of Halloween in 1895, a man named William Kinney (also called "Texas Jack") met his horrible fate near the building? Kinney was murdered by a man named William Wroth (also called "Omaha Bill") in front of the Gold Leaf Saloon, where Wroth was working. The two men were enemies for a long time, but on Halloween night, they could no longer ignore their differences. After a heated argument, Omaha Bill drew his pistol, aimed his gun at Texas Jack, and shot him three times. The second bullet soared through Jack's heart, killing him

instantly. Bill's wife, Della Stone, stood by frozen in fear.

Omaha Bill was immediately arrested by officer James Sipprell. He was taken to the jail, where he sat with a $10,000 bail fine. He was found guilty of manslaughter and sentenced to ten years. Could the ghost in the city jail be that of Omaha Bill? Or maybe it is the spirit of Texas Jack seeking revenge for his untimely death?

Employees working in the building have experienced another very strange phenomenon. When counting the daily cash register receipts, money seems to disappear and just as quickly reappear! More than one employee has experienced this. Coins will magically disappear right from under a person's eyes. It seems that the ghost is playing a fun game. Or maybe it is a former prisoner who was a thief or pickpocket in the 1890s?

The most recent ghost seen in the basement of the Marks Building is not connected to the jail or even the building at all. It's believed that the old lady who haunts this place is here because of her favorite chair. The story goes that a man who works here purchased a beautiful antique chair with plans to reupholster and sell it. As he was working on another project, he saw an old lady sitting in the chair, which he had placed in the hall. He turned to tell her that no one was allowed in the basement except tenants and employees. He thought she had accidentally wandered down to the basement because she got lost or needed help. He called out to her. Then he set his tools down on his work bench and wiped his hands. When he turned back to the woman in the chair, she was gone! He searched all through the halls for the woman, but he never found her.

Startled, the man returned to his work, pretending the event never happened. A few days later, he saw the old lady sitting in the chair again. He simply said, "Hello," to her and smiled. She warmly smiled back.

He decided that the chair had come with a ghost. He no longer desired to reupholster the chair. Some things are better just left the way we find them.

The 1886 Haunted Maughlin Mansion

The Maughlin Mansion at 707 Fourth Street is one of the most fascinating and beautiful estates in all of Snohomish. It was built by Joseph and Mary Maughlin, who came from Ohio in 1886. The Maughlin brothers soon built the nearby Maughlin Brothers Mill that by 1901 employed 80 men. Several generations of the Maughlin family lived in it until the 1920s.

The towering mansion is perched high above the street level, just as it was in 1886. The bell tower is one of the most fascinating features of the mansion. The home slightly resembles a set from a horror movie, except that it is *so* beautiful.

The mansion sat vacant for many years. Local kids would hold séances and use Ouija boards inside, hoping to invoke spirits of the dead. Kids would challenge each other to a good scare by seeing who could stay in the frightening home the longest. Parents would warn their children to stay away from it.

The city threatened to tear the house down.

In 1992, local children's book author and illustrator Rebecca Dickinson stumbled across an advertisement for the sale of the home. She

quickly drove out to see the crumbling beauty and fell in love with it. She decided to make an offer on it. Strangely, it was Halloween day when she took possession of her new home.

She has restored, decorated, remodeled, and added on to the home for decades. After many, many years of hard work (and lots of money), the home is close to its former glory.

Now its interior features velvet curtains, elegant furniture, and beautiful details. People walking by linger on the sidewalk just to admire the grand home. It has become a local curiosity and source of fascination. The huge and captivating home is nothing less than magnificent.

But inside the mansion, strange things lurk in the dark corners and large rooms. It has earned the nickname "Haunted House on the Hill."

During the remodel, Rebecca experienced many strange things. The sounds of heavy footsteps upstairs, faint whispers, odd music, and odors of a woman's perfume and cigars...she has even experienced doors opening, closing, and locking and unlocking by themselves! She has seen eerie faces peering down the stairs. She has heard ghostly music and voices coming from upstairs when no one else is in the home.

One of the most eerie stories took place in the "Monkey Room." Rebecca calls it this because of the monkey wallpaper in the room.

During the remodel, workers found a huge wooden beam in the room that needed to be replaced. As they pulled it out, they discovered a large, partially rotten wooden box. It looked like a coffin! The box was too difficult to remove, so Rebecca told the men to just leave it. Was it an old coffin or simply a large, wooden box? Since the workers did not remove the box, no one knows if a skeleton was inside!

Odd knocking noises come from underneath the Monkey Room. Are they made by sounds a ghost trapped in the coffin?

There is another possibility. Rumors tell of a young man who hanged himself in the bell tower. The legend goes that a young couple was arguing up in the tower room. After a brief struggle, she stormed out of the house, leaving him alone. He was so sad and desperate, he hanged himself in the bell tower room. The girl eventually returned and found her love dead.

Rebecca frequently sees shadowy figures in the bell tower. Is this the ghost of the boy who hanged himself?

Rebecca's favorite ghost story came from her sister, an engineer who does not believe in spirits. The front door to the mansion used to be the entry to the old payroll office. (This was a leftover part of the former Maughlin Brothers Mill.)

Rebecca had the door nailed shut until she could get it fixed. One night, Rebecca's sister came to pick up her children. All the doors were locked, so she walked around the side of the house to look for an open door.

When she came back to the front door—the one that is normally nailed shut—it was wide open! She figured Rebecca had unlocked it and gone back to bed.

When the sisters discussed it the next day, Rebecca was shocked. She hadn't unlocked the door! She checked the front door, and it was *still nailed shut*! They both decided that

perhaps a friendly, motherly spirit had opened to door so that Rebecca's sister could gather her children. After all, ghosts can be kind and helpful, too.

The Miserable Man and His Fiddle

Fiddler's Bluff is a gorgeous area on the south side of Snohomish near the haunted Kenwanda Golf Course. The rolling hillside was once covered with tall pine trees leading all the way down to the nearby Snohomish River. There was a logging camp on the bluff where lumberjacks would cut down the towering trees for timber. An active railroad track for the Northern Pacific Railway came through this way. Several men are said to have died on those tracks; some by accidents, some possibly by murder.

The hillside is said to be haunted by the ghost of William Jamieson, a cook at the

logging camp. With the town booming, lumber was in demand for the construction of housing and railroad buildings. Being right on the river, it was convenient and easier to float the logs down the river than to pull them by horses or oxen. Untamed Snohomish had a good selection of tall trees. In1864, the area near Snohomish produced *millions* of feet of lumber, all cut by hand. Can you imagine cutting a big, tall tree (that was hundreds of years old) down with just a long saw? Two men would pull the saw back and forth at the base of the tree, praying it would not fall the wrong way or snap at the base. Working in the camp was extremely dangerous, and many men died in a split second due to accidents.

The hungry loggers needed to be fed, and Jamieson was one of the men employed to do it. He purchased land bordering the Snohomish River on the bluff in 1867. He soon built a small shack there. He was a grouchy man who never had any friends and didn't care to make any. He spent most of his life alone. His only companion was his fiddle. Whenever he wasn't cooking, Jamieson would sit on a stool by the river and play. Those who heard him play said his talent didn't match his passion for the instrument. He wasn't a good fiddler. People in passing boats would holler at him to stop. The sound of his fiddle hurt their ears!

Jamieson became depressed. He was lonely and sad. He stopped playing his fiddle because of all the complaints about it. He had no way to pass the time. One night, his sadness got the best of him, and he took his own life.

His neighbor Bobby Hughes found his body. Feeling sorry for Jamieson, Hughes buried the poor man on the bluff. His canoe and fiddle were sold to pay for his coffin. Hughes made a makeshift grave marker with the epitaph "Born in Misery, Lived in Misery, Died in Misery."

The wooden marker is long gone. The whereabouts of Jamieson's grave is unknown. Big houses clutter the once barren hillside. Perhaps one is even built over the poor fiddler's grave!

Locals say that late at night, if the wind is just so, you can hear the faint sounds of a poorly played fiddle. Jamieson's musical talents did not improve in his afterlife.

Jamieson shares the bluff with another ghost. A woman can be seen on the back nine of former Kenwanda Golf Course. She wears flowing dresses and is very beautiful. Some believe she is the spirit of Wanda,

the former owner of the golf course. Wanda loved this place with all her heart. She and her husband, Ken Harris, built the golf course off Fiddler's Bluff in 1963, naming it for both their first names combined. People who live near the now-closed course often see her spirit roaming and dancing on the well-manicured grass. Employees of Kenwanda reported seeing her

ghost near the clubhouse, too. Was Wanda still making sure her golf course is being properly cared for? If you are in the area, keep your eyes open for Wanda. You just might spot her in this place she loved.

Haunted Cemeteries of Snohomish

Nothing is scarier than a cemetery... except maybe a cemetery at night! Snohomish has several haunted cemeteries and even a few creepy areas that *used to* be cemeteries.

Some think Maltby Cemetery is the most haunted of all. In fact, it's said one of the most haunted sites in the entire state of Washington! What is so frightening about Maltby Cemetery? It is home to the notorious "Thirteen Steps to Hell," a cement staircase descending to an underground crypt.

According to legend, if you descend the stairs at night, you will lose your mind by the time you get to the very last step. Does some strange paranormal activity take place on the way down? Or do you lose your mind because you are so afraid? There is no clear answer.

Many have attempted to walk the steps. Several have succeeded. Those who have made it to the bottom say they felt light-headed, panicky, and sick to their stomachs. Almost scared to death. *Sounds fun, huh?*

Some say the steps were once part of an underground burial tomb for a wealthy Snohomish County family. But who was this family? Why did they design an underground burial plot? What were they afraid of?

The underground mausoleum might have been a way to prevent grave robbers from disturbing the dead. In the early days of Snohomish, grave robbers were a common problem. When someone died, robbers would show up a few days after the burial to dig up the caskets. They would open the coffins and steal jewelry off dead bodies. Grave robbers were even known to dig up coffins in order

to steal the actual bodies! They would then sell the bodies to medical scientists who were trying to discover cures for diseases or study the human anatomy. This is still illegal today.

In the 1990s, the famous Thirteen Steps to Hell were covered over by a big slab of concrete.

The owners of the graveyard grew tired of ghost hunters and vandals toppling the headstones, performing rituals, and littering the grounds. The steps may be covered, but there's plenty more spooky stuff happening in Maltby Cemetery.

The sounds of a baby crying have been heard at night. Surely there's not a baby lying about in the cemetery! Full-bodied ghouls have been caught both with cameras and with the naked eye. Images of wispy white shadowy figures have been captured on film as they move around above the grave markers. Round orbs of white light sometimes float above a tombstone and then quickly "fly" away. Some say they have heard creepy moans and grunts coming from the bushes when no one else is around.

The cemetery is now closed to the public. But when it was open, there were several rusty old vehicles abandoned on the side of the road nearby. Local residents said that anyone driving to the cemetery would be run off the road by an unseen force. Others claim a big, black 1920s-style car with a phantom driver would

run cars off the road. Are the abandoned cars part of the Maltby Cemetery legend or simply forgotten junk cars? A few of the rusty cars still remain, almost covered and hidden under blackberry bushes, moss, and fallen leaves.

Some said that after they visited the cemetery, their cars would no longer start. They were stuck in the graveyard in a stalled car. It was as if some peculiar energy zapped their batteries preventing them from leaving. A dense fog would surround the car, coiling in from nowhere, slowly fading as the passengers remained frozen in fear. After a few terrifying minutes, the fog would slowly roll away, and the vehicles engine would eagerly turn on, as if nothing had ever been wrong.

Just down the road from the cemetery, the spirit of a woman called the "Lady in Blue"

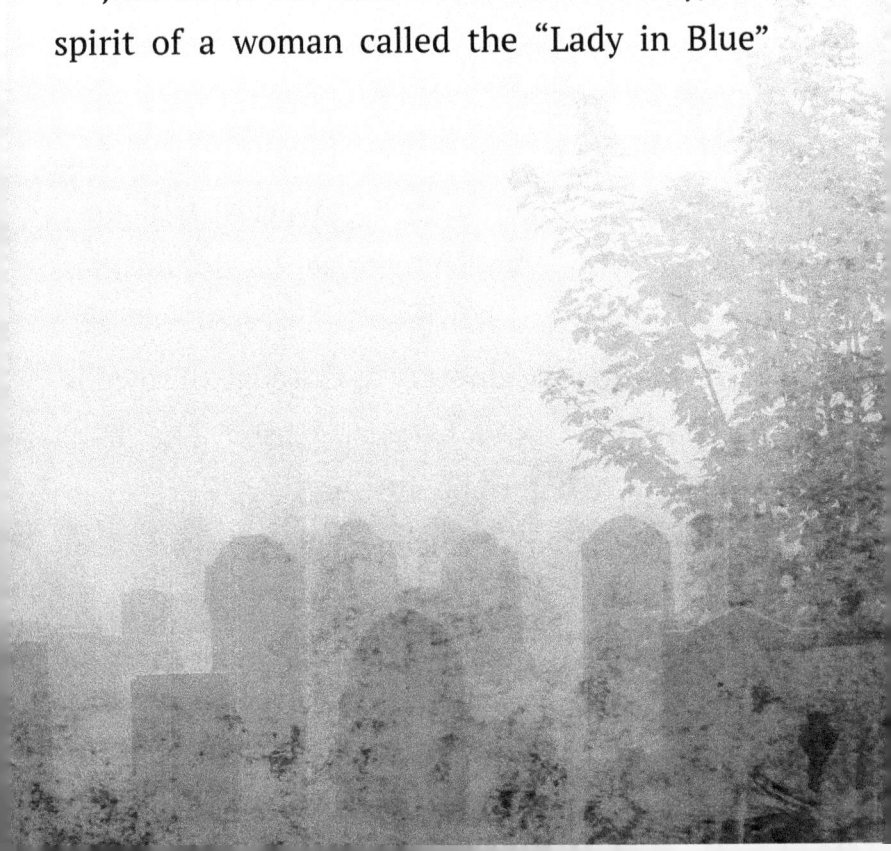

haunts Maltby, walking hand in hand with the ghost of a small boy. Joggers and drivers have seen the ghosts, walking lazily along the road, as if out for a Sunday stroll. Who is ghostly pair? Did they die in a car crash on that road? Or are they the ghosts of a wife and son who are visiting a deceased husband and father in the Maltby Cemetery?

No one knows. The Maltby Cemetery is almost impossible to find today. Markers have been removed, and signs taken down. The ghosts that linger in the graveyard will now have to find something else to do besides scare people!

The Pioneer Cemetery at the edge of town is also haunted. *And for a good reason*. The dead people there had to be moved.

The original Pioneer Cemetery was on Second Avenue at the Pilchuck River Bridge. Townspeople began burying their dead there as early as 1876. By 1885, around 1,020 pioneers and Native Americans found their final resting place there ... that was until the 1940s when construction of a new road began. Workers unearthed many old skeletons. Horrified, they stopped digging immediately. Why were these graves not marked? Because some markers were so old, they had disintegrated. Only the dead knew where they were buried.

But the costly road was already in process, so the bodies would simply have to be moved to another location. Around 111 of the 1,020 bodies found new burials. Ghost hunters claim they have contacted the spirits of the individuals

who were buried at the site, and they are *not* happy! Investigators claim they have captured eerie voices of spirits on their special equipment. The ghosts are mad that just their headstones were moved and not their actual bones. Local rumors even suggest that many of the bodies were secretly buried in a mass grave, their individual identities forever forgotten. About 15 of the grave markers were moved across the new road to the small plot of land next to the 1875 Kikendall log cabin (near the Collector's Choice restaurant on Cypress Avenue). Other bodies were transferred to the GAR (Grand Army of the Republic) Cemetery. Since many of the dead did not have headstones or the old headstones had rotted away,

the identity of some of the dead remains unknown.

Many believe it is bad luck to move a body after it is buried. Is that why so many strange things have happened since the bodies were relocated?

Glowing and swirling white lights have been seen at the cemetery at night. Some have seen a hand-held lantern moving slowly back and forth as if being carried by an invisible hand. Phantom odors of smoke and odd perfume waft from the graves at the Pioneer Cemetery, their scents detected by unsuspecting visitors.

The GAR Cemetery is a few miles from Snohomish and was originally a Civil War cemetery. Construction began in 1898, and it finally opened in 1901. Hundreds of local veterans and prominent Snohomish pioneers are buried here. Almost a thousand soldiers are buried in Snohomish County, their proud souls at rest forever there after fighting horrible wars. These veterans are just a small portion of the many soldiers that fought for our country, but their ghostly energy is enough for a whole army!

Over 3,000 boys from Snohomish and Everett fought in World War I. Not all of them came back. Now visitors say they see ghosts in World War I–era clothing walking amongst the gravestones at GAR. Did other souls of soldiers return to their beloved home in Snohomish to finally rest in peace? Are their spirits looking for brothers of war, searching for their tombstones? It would be impossible to know the identity of the phantom soldiers that roam the grounds. If you visit the beautiful cemetery, be prepared to spend a few hours. It is quite large. Maybe if you keep your ears and eyes open, you might just see the ghost of a soldier!

When remains from the road construction were moved to the GAR cemetery, reports of paranormal activity there increased even further. Are the skeletons and souls of the dead restless because they have been disturbed? Are they angry and confused because their identity was lost in the shuffle?

The Haunted Corn Mazes and Farms

Halloween is a very spooky time of year everywhere, but especially in Snohomish. Local farmers love to create challenging corn mazes for visitors to come and explore. But the corn mazes are not all fun and games.

In the middle of many acres of corn fields, huge spiders cling to the dried leaves, their webs stretching from one stalk to another. The tall leathery corn stalks seem innocent enough until you are in the middle of the maze and don't know which way to turn. If you take a wrong turn, you might never get out, and the ghosts in the maze will steal your soul! Or so they say . . .

Is this just a legend or is there any truth to the story?

There are two important haunted farms in Snohomish: the Thomas Family Farm and Stalker Farms. Scary happenings take place here all year round.

Spirits are said to haunt the Thomas Family Farm fields. In 1935, brothers Sam and Dean Thomas started and ran a packing plant on the family farm that would provide meat for locals.

One horrible day in 1975, poor Sam lost his life when he got tangled up in one of the machines. His body was ripped in half, and he was killed instantly. Some reports suggested foul play; others claim it was truly just an accident. Is there truth to this story? Or is it simply hype to promote the haunted attractions? No one knows the true story.

Stalker Farms is another local farm that's said to be haunted and thrives on scary activities. From the highway, Stalker Farms at 8705 Marsh Road looks peaceful, with its red barn and rolling fields. But locals tell stories of the hauntings in the area.

The Stalker Farms legend tells of a man named Jebediah Slasher, a preacher man who was a cousin of the family who lived there. Although he was supposedly a Christian minister, he secretly held Celtic pagan beliefs. The ritual of Samhain was important to him. That's the pagan fall festival of the dead (which falls on Halloween night). During this celebration, spirits of this world and the underworld mingle and allow the *Aos Sí* (the "spirits" or "fairies") to easily visit this world.

On a cold Halloween night over 100 years ago, Jebediah mysteriously went missing while walking through the cornfield. Locals thought

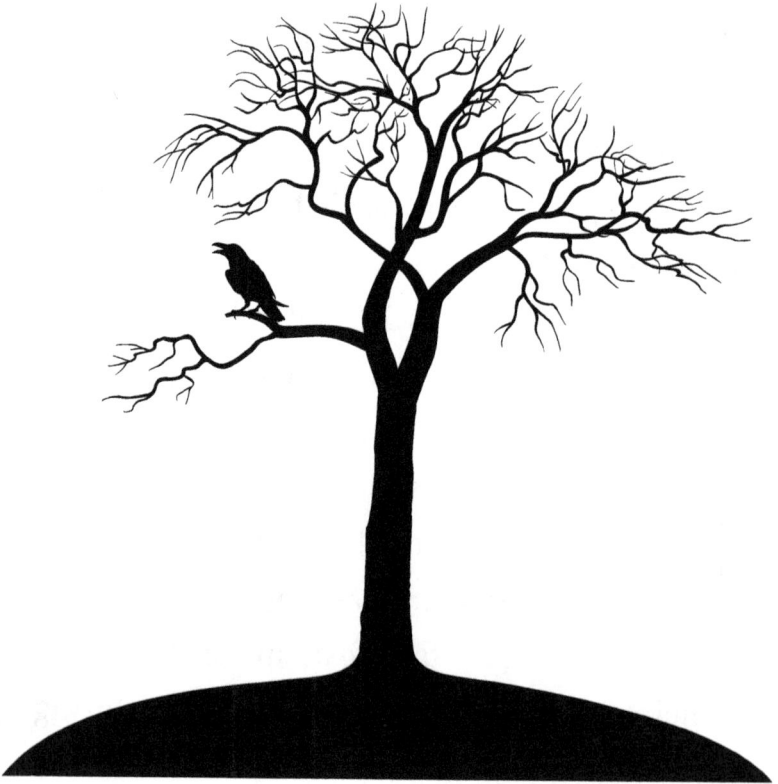

he ran away to spread his spiritual beliefs to people who believed in his message. Others say he was murdered by an unknown attacker and now his spirit seeks revenge . . .

Each year, Stalker Farms creates a new and elaborate corn maze to entice those who want to be scared and try their luck to see if they can escape.

Bizarre sightings of tiny fairies and bright glowing orbs have been seen in the fields. Strange noises can be heard coming from inside the corn mazes. Stalks move on their own, as if someone or something unseen, is walking through the maze. Weird noises have been heard late at night in darkness. Is the angry spirit of Jebediah to blame?

But something even more evil haunts the fields. Stalker Farms is the scene of a creepy story involving a missing clown. Yes, a clown. Could this farm get any creepier?

Sometime in the 1930s, a clown named Pogo ran away from a traveling circus to seek adventure on his own. He hit the road with a new show called Pogo's Playhouse. They say his first (*and last*!) stop was in Snohomish. As he set up his tent for his opening show on the edge of what is now Stalker Farm, there was a sense of excitement in town.

Everyone was eager to enjoy Pogo's show. But his tent remained empty, and the clown never took the stage to perform his act. In a way, Pogo's last curtain call was to mysteriously disappear from sight, never to be seen or heard from again. Many clown-loving locals were confused and wondered what on earth happened to him.

His body was never found, and there's no further information about him. No news articles were ever written about his disappearance. Who was Pogo? What was his real name? What happened to him? It was as if Pogo had performed his own vanishing act.

Now the eerie ghost of a clown can be seen haunting the fields of Stalker Farm. The spirit appears with a bright red nose, white painted face, and baggy clothes. Don't lose your way in the corn maze. You might feel the cold, gloved hand of Pogo the Clown touching your arm or hear the faint squeak of his rubber nose coming from the distance. *And there's nothing funny about that!*

Railroad Ghosts

The railroad tracks that run through town are still used daily by Amtrak and Burlington Northern Railroad. These trains frustrate commuters as they wait for a train to pass when they really need to get to work on time. But as they sit trapped on the only two roads that lead into Snohomish, they might pass the time by looking for a ghost!

Several spirits haunt the train tracks. Late at night, the eerie sounds of screeching metal on metal rings through the midnight air, as if a phantom train is desperately trying to stop to avoid running over someone. Although very unsafe, it used to be common for men and women to walk the tracks.

A local named Lyle who lives near the railroad tracks by Fiddler's Bluff announced to locals, "They hardly ever run a train on the tracks by my house, but I can hear the faint blow of an unknown whistle and the creaky, metal scarping sound of the trains near my place late at night. Sometimes I get up and look out my window hoping to see an actual train so I can tell myself I am not losing my mind, but there is no train running."

Pilchuck Jack (known as the "King of the Pilchucks ") was the last chief of the Pilchucks, a small tribe that fished at the water's edge of the Snohomish River. He was the best-known local resident to be killed on the train track. One dark night in 1905, Jack was walking the tracks that led from Snohomish to the nearby town of Cathcart.

The chief was extremely tired and not paying attention to his surroundings. He stopped for a few minutes to catch his breath and rest. Unfortunately, he sat down on the tracks and fell asleep! He slept so soundly that

even the roaring blare of the trains whistle could not wake him up. The beloved Chief Pilchuck was killed instantly as the train ran over his body. His wife, Princess Julia, was heartbroken. Now the ghost of Pilchuck Jack can been seen sitting on the tracks where he met his tragic death that night so long ago.

A man named William Romines was killed by the train that ran through town. His ghost wanders the railroad that runs between Skykomish and Snohomish. Romines came to Snohomish in the fall of 1872 with high hopes of becoming a hotel proprietor. He bought the Riverside Hotel on Maple Street from John Low for $1,500. Five years later he also purchased the wharf near the hotel and

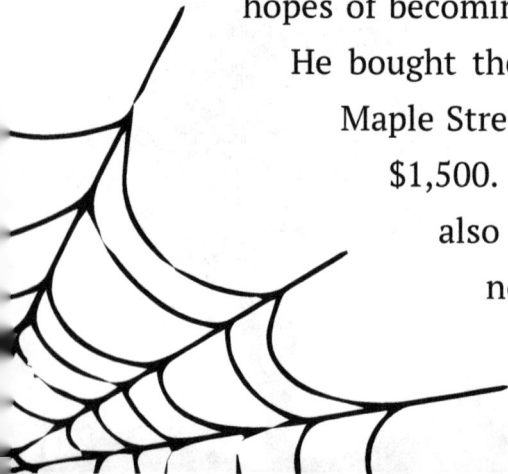

sold logging supplies. Financial troubles soon plagued Romines. His mental health declined. He moved to Skykomish in 1892. There, he came to be known by the nickname Uncle Billy. He died on the tracks while walking from the county farm to Snohomish. Now his confused ghost walks along the tracks trying to get back home.

Other Snohomish Haunts

HARVEY THE PEEKER

At Fred's Rivertown Alehouse on First Street, the ghostly face of a man casually peeks from behind a door, scaring employees. The sounds of heavy footsteps come from another room when no one else is there. As the crew is cleaning up for the night, glasses fly off shelves, thrown by a pair of unseen hands!

These are just some of the things the employees at Fred's Alehouse have to deal with on a daily basis. *What is even stranger than that*? These weird things don't even scare some of the employees anymore. They have become so used to the bizarre events that when something odd happens, they simply say to the ghost, "Cut it out, Harvey!"

In 1911, the building that now houses Fred's Alehouse was known as the Gem Saloon. It was the scene of many bar fights and much gun slinging and illegal gambling. That same year, a devastating fire burned most of the historic district to the ground, including the Gem. One man was reported to have been killed in the flames but was later discovered ordering breakfast in a café safe and sound.

Today, the old saloon has more than great food. It also has a ghost. The spirit restaurant crew calls him Harvey, but his nickname is "the Peeker." Why? Because everyone always sees him peeking from behind things or from behind a door. The sight of his head pops in and out from all over the place!

Harvey also loves to knock glasses and objects off the shelves. Annoyed workers have to pick up items that Harvey the Peeker

pushes to the ground. And Harvey isn't picky. He doesn't care *what* he tosses to the ground. His invisible hand strikes any object that he wants, moving it or pushing it off the shelf, table, or counter. No one knows why Harvey does these things. Maybe he just likes getting the attention.

When workers are alone in the building early in the morning or late at night, they hear someone walking over a heavy metal grate near the kitchen. It is a very distinct sound that sends chills down their spines because they are *alone* in the building! There is no logical reason that noise should be heard.

Other people have been touched by Harvey. He likes to playfully grab people's clothes as they walk by. Some mistake his good-humored attempts to have fun as something evil, but it's not.

Harvey the Peeker is just having a good time—at everyone else's expense!

THE GHOST IN THE BASEMENT

Since 1927, many different businesses have occupied the building at 1107 First Street. It has been an antique store, a pizza place, and a bicycle shop among other things. Inside the two-story structure there's a long, wide set of stairs that leads to the basement. People get the feeling that they should not go down there. If they *do* have to go down there, they soon come running back up to the safety of the main floor!

Employees report that they feel like someone is watching them, and they look over their shoulder to make sure no one is there. Some say they feel as if someone is grabbing at their legs as soon as they start to walk back up the stairs. Maybe the ghost doesn't want to be alone in the basement. Then why doesn't it move up the stairs to the main level? Is the spirit trapped in the basement unable to move? Did someone get killed down there a long time ago? No one knows. Perhaps someday someone will discover who the ghost is that lurks in the darkness of the basement of the building. Until then, it is a mystery.

The Snohomish River Legends

The murky, cold Snohomish River runs along the south side of town. The narrow waterway canal that runs east to west has been both a blessing and a curse. Several stories and legends are told about the river. It has killed several people, dragging them down into the freezing water: Thomas MacIntosh in 1882, Dan O'Neil in 1885, and Jesse Dutcher in 1887.

The unpredictable river has flooded the area multiple times over the years, destroying homes and killing livestock. During the floods, the water rises so quickly there is no time to prepare. Over 3,000 cows and horses died from drowning during these floods. The spirits of these animals can be seen off and on in the farmer's fields and people's pastures. Some have spotted a horse lazily grazing in the sun, raising its head as if to look up at the observer then disappear! Can animals come back as spirits? Many people claim to have seen their beloved pets return to their side in times of stress or sorrow, as if to comfort their old masters. Others swear that they have heard the meow of a deceased cat, the bark of a dog, or even the whinny of a horse. Perhaps the grieving owners simply miss the pet so much that their minds are playing tricks on them.

Or is it possible that animals can come back into this world to visit their owners?

Two spirits can be seen late at night along the river. One is a Native American man. The other is a male riverboat captain.

During the late 1800s, the river was a main source of food, supplies, and travel for town folk and the Snohomish people. The grisly legend of Chief Patkanim has been told around many campfires. Chief Patkanim was a fierce

and strong warrior who would do anything to protect his town and people. He loved the white settlers, and they loved him. Around 1885, Chief Patkanim raged a long battle against other hostile tribes. For ten exhausting hours, the Snohomish warriors fought, killing nine men.

During another battle, Chief Patkanim fought two men, stabbing them to death, and then hung them from a nearby tree. He displayed their bodies as a warning to anyone else who wanted to mess with him. Later, he chopped off their heads. From that day on, no one messed with Chief Patkanim.

His restless spirit still walks along his beloved river, protecting local people from beyond the grave. Dressed in traditional garb, his ghost has been seen down by the water by people standing above on the bridge on Airport Way road. In the blink of an eye, Chief

Patkanim's ghost appears, and in the next instant, he is gone. It is considered good luck if you see Chief Patkanim. A statue is now erected in Everett in his honor.

The river also hosts the ghost of none other than riverboat captain Charles Low. The Low family was a very important part of early Snohomish history. Charles's parents were two of the original pioneers of Snohomish, then called Cadyville. (The town name was changed to Snohomish in 1871.) Captain Low purchased two boats to run on the Snohomish River: the *Nellie* and the *Monroe*. Captain Low loved nothing more than cruising along the beautiful river in one of his boats. Everyone in town respected and admired the captain. He was a hard worker and enjoyed being part of his community.

Then, in 1887, Captain Low died suddenly. The townspeople were shocked and saddened by his death. People noted that Captain Low had a premonition of his upcoming demise and had recently visited a psychic named D.J. Stansbury. Later, it was said that the captain somehow sent a private message to Stansbury on a chalk slate, so it was never properly recorded before its erasure. Could the captain really send a message after his death?

The ghost of Captain Low can be spotted along the river he loved so much while he was alive. His stately figure, complete with a captain's hat, stands proud on his phantom boat as it slowly cruises the water. In death, he continues his mission of providing safe travel and transportation to the citizens of Snohomish.

Perhaps if you stand on the bridge at the west side of town long enough, you will spot either the ghost of Chief Patkanim or Captain Low. If you do, wave at them—they would love it!

You've read just a few of the stories of those who haunt Snohomish. But the best way to learn about the ghosts here is to go and meet them for yourself!

Author **Deborah Cuyle** has written almost a dozen other books on haunted places and towns. She currently lives in her own haunted house in Wallace, Idaho. She loves swapping ghostly tales with her family and friends while nestled around a bonfire.

Check out some of the other Spooky America titles available now!

Spooky America was adapted from the creeptastic Haunted America series for adults. Haunted America explores historical haunts in cities and regions across America. Each book chronicles both the widely known and less-familiar history behind local ghosts and other unexplained mysteries. Here's more from *Haunted Snohomish* author Deborah Cuyle: